Let It Sustain You

Emma K. Shockley

Copyright © 2026 by Emma K. Shockley

All rights reserved.

ISBN-13: 979-8-9945991-9-8 (Paperback edition)

ISBN-13: 979-8-9945991-2-9 (Ebook edition)

No part of this book may be reproduced in any form or by any electronic or mechanical means, including information storage and retrieval systems, without written permission from the author, except for the use of brief quotations in a book review.

Dedication, or:
Letter to a Mayflower

This life will be wonderful,
and there will be moments of hilarity that split your sides.
The passion will be of an intensity you cannot yet conceive of,
and sometimes a fruit will taste so flavorful
it will bring tears to your eyes.
You need not fear despair -
it will pass,
it will pass, and
the sharp edge of pain will reveal a softness
so sublime
you will realize you've been
god all along.
When you can feel no more and the numbness takes over,
celebrate, little flower.
You will be resplendently human in every moment.
And the friendships,
oh, the love...
the excitement and delight I carry with me now
I carry for you,
a warm flame on cold nights
which will guide you home to yourself every time.
You will return to being lost over and over,
and you will find yourself again and again.
You will never be the same after each thing happens,
and you wouldn't change that for the world,
wouldn't conceive of attempting to undo this

*Becoming.
You won't ever dare -
you will just dance madly,
because you will be mad. And
you will dance freely
because you are free,
free as only you could ever be.*

Contents

I

Alien

In Pursuit of Something More	5
Luminosity Unknown	6
$500 Fine	7
American Abroad ‖ Migrant Melody	8
Enemy of the State	13
Wanderer	14
Explanation	15
Recipe for Sticking to Your Values	16
Instrument of Insignificance	17
Weltschmerz	18
Rewilding	19
What Amelia Knew	20
That Which Flickers, or: Solidarity Song	21
This Life Is Not My Own	22
Witness	24
Hurtling, Stuttering, Lurching, Stop Me	25
I Miss You	26
And So It Goes	27
Triple Dog Dare	28
Abide	29
Frühling, 2025	30
Weaver	31
When a Person Is a Portal to Grief	32
Space Walk	33

Demon

Profusion	37
Into the Belly of the Beast	38
Twisted	39
Askew	40
Reasons to Leave	41
Double Checking	42
Intrusive Thought	43
Spiteful Diver	44
Forest Fire	45
Unmenschlich	46
Keep Them Away	47
I Feel Like a Shell of Myself	48
SN	49
The Strength of Your Love	50
Nonverbal	51
Never Quite Right	52
The Myth of Linear Necessities	53
Lessons From Water	54
Vessel	55
Undulate	57
What I Like	58
Message From My Future	59
Reasons to Stay	60
Gossamer Grit	61
This Poem Has So Many Commas	62
This Is Suicide Prevention, Otherwise Known As Living	63

Freak

I don't want anyone to touch me anymore I'm serious, no one no one no one.	67
Drip Drip	69
Searching for the Funk	70
Awake	71
Decompose	72
Stable Rollercoaster	73

A Response to the Statement:	74
Deity Reborn	76
Angel	77
Cornucopia	78
Echoes	79
Alles Gut	80
Schmetterling	81
Heavy Breathing	82
Queer Love	83
Devotee	84
Hallowed Be Thy Name	85
Chrome Lighthouse	86
The Clarity of Delusion	87
There Are No Lines to Read Between, Only Continuity	88
Confessions	89
Gradient	91
Shot Through the Heart	92

Witch

Sonnenschutz	95
Relativity	96
Vampire	97
Undertones	98
Princess Pomegranate	99
Middle of Nowhere	100
Cave Woman	101
The Biggest Drops I Ever Saw	102
After the Apocalypse	103
Serpent	104
Gemini's Spiral	105
Check In	106
Thurauen, Equal Parts Day and Night	107
The Inverse of Half-Life	109
Night Terror	110
Protected	111
To Exist	112

Reality Check 113
Participation Trophy 114

II

Blood

Them, Which is to Say: Me 119
Water Cycle 122
Journey 123
Succession 124
Not to Be Seen 125
Innocent Crimes 126
Your Legacy Will Be Your Curse 127
When My Mom Braids My Hair 128
Me, Which is to Say: Us 129
Another Chance 130
Mushrooms Preserved in Honey 131
Transcendence of a Trilobite 133
Daisy Chain 135
Nova 136

Death

Where and What and When 139
Hecate's Disciple 140
Uncreated 141
Obsessed 142
Hallelujah 143
Devastation and Delight 144
Event Horizon 145
Psalm 146
It's All So Ominous 147
Memento Mori 148
Necroromance 149
Recounting of a Prophecy 150
Magic Trick 151
Alchemist 152
Impossible Anatomy 153

Autumn	155
Remember me.	156
Heaven	157
Untitled	158
In Every Life	159

Love

Cincinnati Spring	163
What Will We Become?	164
Not Enough	165
Loving Vapor	166
Spacetime	167
How Much Longer Does Venice Have?	168
Clay Canaries	169
888	170
Undercurrent	171
A Griot and a Girl	172
Bear Trap	173
The Opposite of Inertia	174
Scoliosis	175
Us, PS	176
Ouroboros	177
Guardian	178
Lovers Tango	179
Lunar Dance	180
Pirate's Frenzy	181
Wave Function	182
Loving You Is Easy	183
We Tend	184
Galactic Garbage Gang	185
Entropy	186
Poem for my Friend	188
Pause	189
Cave Futurism	190
Faith Is Ours for the Meaning Making	191
Brace for Impact	193
Inevitable by Design	194

Attic black-figure amphora, c. 530 BCE	195
I Think of You Whenever I Marvel	197
Mr. Newton Knew Something of Love	198
Non-Inertial Reference Frame	200
Axiom	201
The Bread We Bake, or: Where Do All the Petals Go	202
Carnivore(s)	204
Love Poem at 00:56, or what I mean to say is	206
Unfolding Incarnate	208
Schmetterling, Pt. II	209
Acknowledgments	211
About the Author	213

I

Alien

In Pursuit of Something More

That crack wasn't always there.
Where did it come from,
and why do I see it just now?

Luminosity Unknown

I spend my days photographing flowers
and listening to the chirps of critters.
What is a lightning bug seen
in the brightness of day?
How could a stranger to these lands
understand its magnificence
when taken only
out of context?

$500 Fine

I am a plastic bottle,
the small parts of me no one sees slowly
poisoning those who drink of me.
And even after you toss me away,
I will take years and years and years to decay,
my presence an aberration to the environment
that once was so pristine.
But who is to blame for
my act of pollution?
All I wanted was to be filled.
I wasn't made to make your home a wasteland.

American Abroad
|| Migrant Melody

I
"He's on the wrong side."
"So many are and they don't even realize it."
Both of us assume we are on the same side but
from our words there's no telling which side we mean.
This is what we've become -
the language of war fumbling from our too-loud tongues like
children playing war,
no conception of the sacrifice battle demands
save for the loss of those who raised us and who live in the
shadow of the deception
they wouldn't rebuke,
the untethered, unhomed confusion
of being not there but there
reducing us to assumption for the sake of
partitioned solidarity.

II
Arrogant consumers, uneducated and unhealthy, what would
we know of the World?
Let me ask you this.
What would you, passive onlooker,
sheltered and comfortable,
know what it means to spin beauty out of the
wreckage of abandonment?
What do you know of wrestling a new way from a

lineage of oppressors
when there is no hope to be found,
when the rest of the world has disowned you despite your
ferocious clamor for
the end to their subjugation?
What do you know of the subtlety of representing a government who does not represent you,
of what it is to live in the belly of the beast that wants to
maim you, disappear you, deny you?
To live without and nevertheless be consumed?
To be buried six feet under and live anyway,
evolving to craft vitality with the worms and heavy metals?
We eat trash and we thrive because we
understand what it means to live
beyond the confines of production,
not machines to be optimized but
walking contradictions who love life and whose will will
always find a way.

III
Show me a map and I will show you deception.
Those of us scattered far and wide know that
borders do not define home,
that a nation is no substitute for the spirit-sustaining camaraderie that is stepping into the
fight for each other.
Hush.
Imaginary lines which divide will never keep us safe.

IV
Do you know what it is to claim a nation with so much blood
on its hands?

What it is to not turn away,
but rather to surrender to a faith in transformation?
The soul-clenching grit required to believe in something better, and then
work for it work for it work for it?
We belong nowhere because the people who reign over us have wrongfully claimed everywhere.
Everyone else hates the effort of
seeing our humanity because it means admitting that
all the parts of themselves they hate are worth fighting for too.
I know less of the sweetness of honey which preserves the goodness of resistance
than most of my comrades
but I listen, I listen, I listen
and I learn,
and it's more than I can say for many of the people who claim to know me because
my ancestors couldn't stand to stay any longer in the place they never left,
the place they still know as home.

V
What does a descendent owe ancestors who watered a land not theirs with the
blood of holy innocents?
Evil deeds begot me and I
am the breaker of cycles,
my ancestor's worst nightmares:
traitor to my inheritance,
childless mother birthing the world they tried to abort.
This is what it means to be pro-life.
American girl, American dream rewritten:

a return of wealth for descendants of ancestors who
watered a land they had no choice but to reclaim indigineity
upon
with blood their own;
free holy lands;
a de-centering.

VI

You do not like our cultures yet you consume our cultures?
You do not like how we wield weapons in the fight we have
been forced to fight, yet you claim karma even as the imperialist machine marches ever closer to your door?
Show me your complaints and I will show you yourself.

VII

I believe in the sanctity of the people,
in the downfall of those who divide us.
I believe in the nuance of separating State from citizen.
I am a shape shifter reborn a thousand times,
that I may fight in every corner against
that which would force-feed us constrictions and
define with no imagination
who we are and what we could become.
I do not turn away because I cannot turn away.
If I do
we are gone,
our future is gone.

VIII

The world wants me to take their disdain with a grain of salt
and then
scatter it across the earth of my first breath,

replicating the ignorance of colonists,
but I have learned
never
to take old salt to a new home.
I flavor a pot of soup bubbling under the stars with this grain
(my most American trait, that I can conjure sustenance from
the curse of another)
and invite you to sit down.
We are on the same side, don't you see?
I yearn for liberation because we are not all free.
I rebuke the illusion of freedom
so many
have been bamboozled by.
I fight for life instead, and
I do not rest until we are all fed.
Come, sit at my table.
Look into my eyes,
star-spangled and thirsty.
Let us together greet the better world already
peeking over the horizon.

Enemy of the State

The women who are displaced
from the loved ones they call home
are the ones who return
with tears made of stars.
Entire constellations
telling the story of their grief,
guiding those who dare look up
when lost.
Yes, we survive and persist,
but there is other fuel besides despair.
Fire will find the will to burn
no matter the kindling.
We need not have been charred at the stake.
It need not have been
so cruel.

Wanderer

In my fall from grace
I found grace,
and speaking of Great Findings -
when you find yourself lost, it bears
remembering:
you need not be found.
You needn't wait, helpless,
a victim to unfamiliarity and uncertainty.
All you need do,
dear one,
is draw the maps to this uncharted territory,
fill the strange constellations you see with
the stories of how they brought you here,
the only place you could possibly be.

Explanation

Some days I don't smile at all and
the sun doesn't remember me.
Words from poems I wrote years ago return to me because they are
spells I conjured for myself here now.
This is witchcraft -
the refraction of time to hold myself alive,
the retraction which follows release
which is really an awakening of something
dormant and deeper.
I am folding in upon myself like the collapse of a woman's chest after betrayal,
like turning a hat inside out only to find it works both ways.
The topography of healing
oneself and the land
is elusive and transient,
that's the point of this poem.
Now that I've given you it, I must say,
I was born to fly
I was born to grow
and how could I become her,
the me who stars whisper secrets to,
if I stayed exactly where my expansion was hindered?

Recipe for Sticking to Your Values

I do not doubt myself,
but I am thorough.
Question the answers, and then
do three more trials.
Take the average,
now wait.
In the silence after observation,
remain steadfast in
your commitment to analysis.
Normalize the data
and do not shy away from
the tedium of calculations,
lest you ever start to accept
what ought never be
permitted.

Instrument of Insignificance

And if we keep on crying
who will catch our souls
as they leak out of our eyes?
Sunday wasn't meant to see this

eat my heart
eat my heart

it is rare and bloody and
I am so alive that I am dying.
I can't stand to bear the possibility
of tomorrow's alphabet because
the State sucked the marrow clean out of me and
all that's left is a
brittle flute
for giants to play.

Where do we go from here?
There is no way

no way

to survive this;
the only way out is through the mouths of our mothers
and the hands of our sisters
which beckon us into tomorrow.

Weltschmerz

Bugs bite me and I let them,
because if it's a creature beyond myself
it's not self harm
(I was a contortionist before I ever wrote poems).
I'm over it all.
Let the world crumble,
let us dig our own massive grave,
too big for our gravity-riddled frames,
too small for the enormity of our foolishness.
Sprinkle seeds over it once the dirt has settled
and
see what our decay allows to blossom,
what fills the space left by the
absence of our stumbling action.

Rewilding

The specificity of a caterpillar stuns.
Small worlds, unknowable unravellings
expanding to shred skin and
contracting to implode structure,
mimic the unbelonging that emerges when we succumb to
the delicacy of our wings.
Purple is purple until it blends into our skin and
the impact is lost in finding ourselves lost.
I feel myself alien against the backdrop of
my context
my context
my context,
meanwhile the caterpillars bubble down until
the perversity of entropy focuses their goop
into gossamer enterprises.
Weariness weighs me down,
and yet
determination hurls me further into an
effervescent,
unseeable dimension,
my innards liquifying,
a soft shell forming around me as the
world carries on and the context shifts,
no matter my delicate metamorphosis
which I return to
again and again and again.

What Amelia Knew

The wind whispers sweet visions to me.
I feel the stirrings of real ambition for the first time in years
and the secrets of the universe
are not so secret after all,
in fact they are plainly written
in the unsolicited kindness of
a stranger and the
unsuspected grace
residing inside.
If I am to fly
I must find the force to
accelerate
to a speed which is not urgent,
but faster than the world spins.
Because don't you see -
if we go with the Earth
the sun need never set.

That Which Flickers, or: Solidarity Song

Lightning bugs and stars
and real lightning and
airplanes in the night sky
all demand my attention,
a twinkling symphony of
electricity and audacity.
The Systems ask:
Who dare display such beauty along
these poisoned, rotting shores,
the stench of waste rising from the summer heat?
What dare light up the world
with wonder
and hope
in times that are dark and fearful?
Us,
they answer with their glimmering, luminous lights.
Us,
I chime in,
my vitality flickering among them.

This Life Is Not My Own

I dreamt of war crimes in Palestine last night.
I protested the violent stabbing of civilians I saw,
went mad from the sound of slicing flesh and
cackling soldiers
and when I named this as evil they covered my mouth and
tortured me.

How many ways are there to rape the righteous?

It starts with the flesh,
a penetration,
a breaking down of the vibrating anger of muscle.
What follows is what is left unspoken -
the degradation of knowing that it is the strength of our love
which triggers their cruelty.
The steadfast clarity of knowing what we stand for
is our crime, condemned by
those who have split their souls and so many bodies.
I revoke their names.
They are already forgotten, cowards.
I instead name the martyrs as the
subjects of my curse
leer and threaten my flesh.

Hind. Mohammad. The families, whole families.

Cut out my eyes, I dare you.

It will not stop me seeing right from wrong,
thousands upon thousands of singing angels
drowning out your attempts to
name hope obsolete.

Kill me. I am more than my fear in the face of your evil.
I cannot die, my imagination for a just tomorrow is legion in
the blood of my comrades.
We will not stop until the balance of growth is restored -
the list of murdered: stagnant.
The number of olive trees: skyrocketing.
Name me Oracle.
I see a free Palestine, the fall of an empire,
fields of poppies as far as the eye can see.

Witness

Flowers bloom atop a bus stop as the people transfer and I
fly by.
What wouldn't I give to feel you beside me,
to trace the curvature of your ribs
and hear you murmur in my ear once again?
Listen, I am writing prophecies from the blood
still within me,
I see the suffering all around and I swear I will
not look away,
I will not look away,
look,
see how the clouds change form.
See how they were never meant to last anyway.

Hurtling, Stuttering, Lurching, Stop Me

Thank me before we?
Do you think we could?
I would, but then what if the edge?
And wouldn't it then,

just
like
that?

We couldn't, we already did, didn't we?
And then, shouldn't be too hard to?
I was taught that.
And the days go by.
And the nights are there too.

And the nights are there too.

I Miss You

The moon stares back at me because
nothing is real.
Nothing is real, except that I am
here without you,
the void which should be you a presence so charismatic,
the nation of my body has sworn allegiance
with all its soldiers.
My gut, which knows this distance is perverse.
My lips, who succumb to gravity's downward grip.
My thighs, which shudder in the chill of the
absence of your hand.
And my heart,
who knows nothing but how to love.
I am listless and restless,
the paradox of your lack a purgatory worse than hell.
Where does she go,
the me that exists only in the safety of your gaze,
when I am left alone these long nights?
How can it be that I remember your fierce love
and the world becomes more beautiful,
the ache in my heart a gnawing roar
powering the awe of this wonderful,
weird
existence?

And So It Goes

The moths will turn back to the moon when
all is said and done,
though I don't think this phrase makes sense.
It could never all be said.
It could never all be done,
though it has certainly all already happened.
The minutes are long and
the years are short
and the longing for a world ascending the horizon
that we will never quite reach
is a blade being sharpened even as
blood seeps through the soil.
I have bathed in waters only I know exist and
I can assure you -
the air between us is a molecular connection
we must never sacrifice.
A vacuum knows no motion
and a clock has no patience for misperception.
The ticks march ever onward.
The past is a present we re-wrap each Christmas
while the drunks keep drinking and the romantics
keep writing,
keep writing,
haunted by some knowing they will
never be able to
fully articulate.

Triple Dog Dare

I caught one of your Thinks and it
blew away before I could write it down.
We are bonded;
and what shall we do now that we're here among
all this beauty,
too tired, perhaps, to take it in?
The orange of the sunset is fleeting and
every carrot is reminiscent of your hands
immersed in cool loam.
Besides that:
where do we keep the things that we
forgot to say when we still had the chance and
everything important that we
can't remember?
Maybe the sound of clinking cutlery in the evening air is you.
Maybe this fresh green smell is my letter to you.
Maybe my vivid dreams are prophecies.
Maybe it will all just be ok?

It will all be ok.

Abide

A cold mandarin after sex
as the colder stars blink through the winter-clear evening air.
The following day I drink warm beverages with the
women in my life and we
talk about how despite the fact that we are always ourselves,
it seems we
have changed.
We have changed and it is winter,
the season of five sleeps,
and I am waiting for the pain to pass me by,
quiet as the world after freshly fallen snow.

Frühling, 2025

There are women crying on the train,
my god there are women crying on the train,
and the wisteria are blooming
halfway across his indigomagenta unhappening.
Let's wait to see what's become of us at the turning of next
season before we
jump to conclusions so irresponsible they
speak for the children without ever having been
children themselves.
Inquisitiveness sustained death last year but
I don't think it can get away with that twice,
otherwise where would asteroids leave their mark?
You think these things are not connected?
You deign to understand patterns that have
not yet become patterns?
You were never so great,
Death never so wise.

I will go to sleep once the heat has cooled,
in the meantime let us loll,
daydream you here with me.

Weaver

These are the days of rustic orange manifestations.

The world is so beautiful it becomes
an assault to our struggle.
Nevertheless, spiderwebs appear overnight
and I am enraptured.
What does it take to spin a home out of
only yourself?
To craft connections between the structures
of your environment,
both architect and construction worker,
supplier and consumer?

Could I let this world devour me too?

I think incessantly of my blood being drained,
limbs compressed under the gossamer warmth
of the strands I have spun
as I grow pale and weak.
It could be that this is what I wanted,
to be both spider and prey.
And it might be that the moths I've caught were

only ever myself

all along.

When a Person Is
a Portal to Grief

I am lightning
and you the thunder that follows.
How many seconds sit between us?

Space Walk

The skies are definitely friendly and we
are probably already dead.
To know the beginning of something is to
know the end,
but what of the middle?
All this happening,
all this living,
is a shoe that fits a bit too snug,
is a bit out of style,
but enough, enough.
Please tread on me
and leave me gasping for air.
Please launch me into space and
let me find my grave there.
I want to know what it is to open my eyes wide
and see nothing but the void blazing with the
brilliance of our star.
I want to feel how it is to be alien, to breathe
among emptiness.
Finally, I am cool enough here to see:
this becoming becomes me.
By now I am out of oxygen and
spinning out.
The sun flashes across my vision like a strobe light.
For a moment it is beautiful -
I see the lives of everyone who ever lived
and I -

Demon

Profusion

This is a poem about rape that's not a trigger warning it's just that if I don't name it now I'll beat around the bush and you could be forgiven for thinking I meant an unpleasantly cold swim a suffocation the collapse of a star the pressure of 20,000 leagues under the sea or maybe you'd think I meant a war my body the battlefield the site of advance and retreat of pain and cries silenced or possibly you could mistake it for a misunderstanding, so many do, so many do and don't even get me started on the blood curdling possibility that you mistake my rape for desire for love for getting caught up in passion red hot as a burning poker as a fire fueled by loss as the tears the tears the tears the tears the tears the tears the tears the tears I don't think we're on the same page about this I don't think we have a shared foundation from which to dialogue how do we do this through the tears the tears the tears the tears the tears the tears the tears the tears?

Into the Belly of the Beast

I spiraled among the stars and in the pulsing light
I smelled earth.
The worst happens

again but differently

and then we keep on living.
Deep in a cave, water drips resolutely
and the breath of the abyss is cold.
Where do we land when we are tossed out like trash?
Where do we go when we
lose ourselves?

Twisted

I am ugly
ugly as they come
ugly on the inside
and I confess that
sometimes it's an enjoyable relief to
abandon the mask of beauty.
I relish in my shadows and
take comfort in the darkest parts of me.
This is my secret -
that here, in the forbidden crevice of
all that is taboo,
I have finally found my refuge.

Askew

There's something bittersweet in the air tonight.
In the climax of summer I dream of autumn,
of things dead and decaying
and of veils ever thinning.
I yearn for a future I will never remember
and I grieve a past lost to the present's mind.
Who would I be, had I known that I had nothing to fear
from a foot dangling over the bed's edge at night?

My demons make me dance
and my demons hide themselves among the
whispers of cracked and dried pages which
crackle as my hands flip feverishly
through them, revealing
the destiny of my curse.
If you could understand my story maybe
this would be gentler.
What could we have rather accomplished in the time
it took me to explain that you are
once again
one of my demons too?

Reasons to Leave

It hurts.
Him. Them. Me.
The shadow on the wall.
The fact that it ends anyway.
Self-determination.
What will happen tomorrow.

Double Checking

If I did it would you still love me?
It could mean anything, but
you know the it that I mean.
I pour a glass of wine and a drop trickles down
the outside of the glass.
Now it is wet.
What of topography clarifies that the inside
is not wet too?
I think of how books and friends keep prolonging my life,
with an honorary mention for flowers.
When I walk in the rain I am dry.
When I lie in your arms I am wet.
Who could say which is love and which
the result of love?
A day is a distance
and so is the expanse of your heart,
red like a cardinal,
fleeting like a hummingbird,
reverberating in my ribcage like
the workday of a woodpecker.
And what of the seasons?
What of hearses?
Could I skip these tediums and return to the question:
if I did it would you still love me?

Intrusive Thought

The smell of rain is heaviest after midnight
when the want of you still
whispers through my cells.

I am devastated
I am devastated
I am devastated

because the loneliness in my body
draws out the words from my mind,
unwilling,
appalled,
yet compelled nonetheless:

end it
end it
end it

lest this unbeing
persist.

Spiteful Diver

I want so badly to be seen as the table you stubbed your
toe on.
Real.
It seems that the harder I try to become tangible to those who
love me,
the more voracious they become in packing me
full to to the brim
with metaphors.

And all the while Atlantis sparkles with dropped jewels and
soft algae.

It isn't very sweet,
to be mythologized to the point of procreation,
to the point of birthing a new me,
just that I may finally be seen as I am.
I'm so good at observing because I know what is is to be
observed.
Who plucked me from my peace and placed me here among
those
so desperate
for legends and lore
that they would rather name me everything besides
what I am?

I found the lost and sunken city years ago.
I will never tell you where it is.

Forest Fire

Bless it all.
Not even nine and I'm lost in my mind.
The devil whispers in my eyes and ears
all the livelong day
and I gush blood from
the pores of my labyrinthine psycho ailments.
Horses couldn't gallop fast enough to escape these fractured lenses,
no rainbow is colorful enough to compete
with the wavelengths my mind makes up.

The past is burning behind me and
the smoke obfuscates my view,
fills my lungs and chokes me.
What will the blessings matter when I'm gone?
We could have danced anyway, though
the chaos of the flames charred me so nice,
and the burning wood smelled so good,
so good.

Unmenschlich

Why do you need to feel me?
All you need to know is
my blood is made of roses
thorns and petals
my breath is made of loam
decay and gemstones
I could let you feel me if you would
stop trying to feel me.
Let me be and then I could be with you,
let me be
let me be.
Your pain pains me.
I don't think this is the place for us.

Keep Them Away

The violence of crushing my teeth into the flesh of a crisp
apple reminds me of the
force I am willing to use to
get to something sweet.
I don't care if the crunch offends;
those who mind have forsaken themselves and forget that
doing this keeps the doctor away.
There was a time when doctors surrounded me,
IV drip, blood drawn ruby red as a wicked apple, miasma of
medicine, sickly skin, fever dream.
There was my child and a choice
and I chose to stay,
a choice that haunts me to this day,
it's why I eat the apples,
it's why sharp lines are so enticing,
it's why some can't stand to bear
being bathed in the light of another -
it's a reminder that it's either this fever dream or the next.
There are some people who resent the prismatic truth that
it's not always both\/and.
Schrödinger is glamorous,
but upon observation even he concedes that sometimes it's
either/\or.
If his cat bit me I would not object, blue rivers flooding red,
the crunch of flesh a warning for the next doctor who dares
approach,
my wound a talisman that can't be denied.

I Feel Like a Shell of Myself

I sit outside because the sound of bugs drowns out the
nonexistent buzzing.
I cannot remember when I last felt delight.
I eat because I must, but still
I eat too little.
I cry because the feelings are so big,
but still I am numb,
I am numb.
I wonder if I have the strength to rebuke mistreatment.
Where have I gone?
Is this really me, the thing left behind
after my sparkle sputtered out?
My strength has always been steadfast, so
where do these questions come from?
I'm too tired to answer them, but still
I lie awake at night,
haunted by memories I start to fear
were only ever ghosts.
Where is my tenacity?
Where is my vivacity?
Won't someone throw me a life vest,
though I fear I may have already drowned?

SN

I've never been one for resisting temptation.
You thought this would be a poem about love
or perhaps simply lust,
but I regret to inform I write rather about the
tipping point,
the point beyond despair from which one cannot return.
I may just be there and
I may just do it -
attempt the temptation of finally taking control.
Finality,
its certainty comforts me, so I let
the erraticism of my internal weather push me to the
precipice of losing control and
here I stand.
Why shouldn't I?
You're already sad.
I could stay a while,
but I could also find relief.
Let me rest.
The sadness may linger, but you will be just fine.
I am with you, always.

The Strength of Your Love

Why won't you let me
kill myself?

Nonverbal

An entire novel stuck and stagnant
behind a dam.
Words ricocheting around inside
faster than the speed of light,
each collision with the container
more painful than rejection,
the echoes of contact
a symphony of infuriating tinnitus.
The tension, yes, that too,
the dull ache of incapability.
See me,
but do not perceive me.
Understand me,
I beg of you.
If you try to touch my essence maybe you will find
the sentences I cannot speak.

How does one escape a room with no doors,
and no light to
prove through perception
that it exists at all?

Never Quite Right

It happens at night.
Minutes stretch into infinity and are gone in
one moment.
I am stuck within the breath before death and the pain
makes me feel so alive,
so alive.
There is too much life inside of me.
Too much emotion,
too much perception,
too many immature, ill-formed, unloveable
sobbing children that could never quite
figure it out.
When we are this messy the moon is red.
When we are so confused roses pierce our eyes.
Watch the blood drip down the stem and
remember:
those who want were not meant for this world.
Those who try face a certain death, and it
happens at night,
it happens at night.

The Myth of Linear Necessities

The symphony of my muscles keeps my bones upright
against their better wishes and
icicles tell a
different tale from Eden.
I've said goodbye to you and found my peace
more times than I care to admit,
only to be pulled ever back by the
tantalizing cocktail
of pheromones and poems which is
so reminiscent of something godly just
beyond my meager perception.

I am overwhelmed so easily, yet
possess a strength few are acquainted with.

Acceptance, kindness, authenticity.
Devotion, commitment, freedom.

Such soft power, such gentle ferocity
swirls through the hot star of this consciousness,
sharp as a molecular blade.

Cut me and I will bleed only tomorrow,
though I've already felt the pain.
I've already felt the pain.

Lessons From Water

When you are still, the world is reflected in you.
Ripples at the surface signal something sunken
deep down below.
There is beauty in the freeze, sustenance in the fall,
relief in the thaw.

Vessel

Living is always a choice,
always a choice.
My heart pumps blood which
wets my veins
and keeps me alive,
keeps me alive.
Where is the discomfort held?
How cellular is this impossible, unending ache,
how atomic this despair?
Perhaps if you split the particles that are me
you will find
The Abyss
in the in between.
So then what of breath,
of the exchange of such gasses as
fill my blood?
When the world becomes me
and I am this world become,
what patience do my cells have for
questions like these?
Death is sometimes a choice,
sometimes a choice.
My lungs make a möbius of me
and in the tradeoff of
rejuvenation and refuse I remember:
the choice is perhaps never mine,
never mine.

I will always be me,
no matter the dis-ease.
The air has always been here.

I am the instrument through which the
choices of creation
flow.

Undulate

Everything is complicated
and nothing is obvious except
loving you,
loving you,
and the controversy of despair keeps me up all night and
down all day.
Desperation descends and
aspiration ascends and
I'm afraid I may only have two dimensions after all.
I'm afraid I may be exactly what I fear.
I'm afraid of my capability to cope,
I cannot go on,
I must go on,
go on and get gone,
it's all I've ever known, to
flee to safety,
but now I step sideways instead of
heeding hierarchy.
The dance is not done,
the stepping stones will be found stubbornly.
I remember:
I can move forward and backward, too.

What I Like

I like to watch the bees.
I like to whisper to the wind.
I like to feel the sun between my toes
and smell decaying compost.
I like to breathe and sit still
and lose track of time,
hours falling into the emptiness of my mind.
I like to remember that the world goes on without me.
I like to remember that I go with the world.

Message From My Future

I will sit with you through this
breathe with me
breathe with me
you are not alone,
though you must feel alone.
I will not complete your tasks,
though I will hold you in
utter compassion
as you do
what must be done.

Reasons to Stay

It's beautiful.
Him. Them. Me.
The shadow on the wall.
The fact that it ends anyway.
Self-determination.
What will happen tomorrow?

Gossamer Grit

I am practicing hope like a workout,
sweating voraciously,
fighting for even a drop of it.
Hope is not simply there -
it is hard earned.

And I am playing hope like a cello,
sweet and haunting,
a beauty brought about by the friction of this
impossible world.

This Poem Has
So Many Commas

The dentist told me that I've been brushing my teeth too hard,
wearing down my gums to further expose bone
at too high a rate.
The bone never complained to me,
so I suppose that in my fervor, I exposed what was ready to be seen, just later,
later.
Maybe the beration was rather about the destruction of the softness which
played a role,
which protected a part of me
that once revealed,
forever changed the landscape of
my expression.
And isn't that just like me,
tending with such intensity to keep myself well
that along the way,
I lose what can never come back.

This Is Suicide Prevention, Otherwise Known As Living

I like to be braless.
I like to go fast.
I like to take it slow.
I like to notice things.
I like stories.
I like that morning stretch where I shake my legs.
I like to create.
I like to connect.
I like passion.
I like what all my senses reveal.
I like looking through windows.
I like my hair.
I don't always like things, and I like that too.
I like to be open.
I like to relax.
I like to change.
I like the possibility of the end.
I like to begin.

I like to begin.

Freak

I don't want anyone to touch me anymore I'm serious, no one no one no one.

The truth is this and I'm not going to pussyfoot about I turn towards the lessons of kink to escort my nervous system through the gruesome monstering bloodbath neuroplasticity catalyzes I find clarity in pain I want my muscles to scream my heart to pound so hard I think I'm dying I want the feedback the dominance the assertion of future me pulling me through the reckoning the laying to rest the worms crawling through me the worms crawling all the way through the earth to pop up in between the wild strawberries your hypnotizing hands pluck god you're beautiful god you're so beautiful I dream of wearing your boxers I dream of exsanguination at your hands I am becoming a cicatrix a role reversal a reverberation a remaking this is a rendezvous no this is submission and there we have it it always comes down to power doesn't it power and control I submit as I dominate myself I dominate myself as I submit to the truth it's like I said before Sunday wasn't meant to see this I was told that if I sin I go to hell that God is watching but I know now that so too is the devil I was told that it takes strength to do what I am doing that I am disciplined no the truth is that I'm only disciplined in the way that people who try to catch lightning in a bottle are and here we stand back at that point which is both implosion and explosion the truth is this and I'm not going to pussyfoot about I think that this interplay is magnificent I think that you are quintessential that if you hummed a lullaby I could hear it from right here just today a baby laughed at me and I sat with my comrade in silence in the city stewing in the summer heat and I want to add that I think our politicians should live in fear now this is the truth I alluded to all along this is the artists spiral I'm not grateful to be alive but I am grateful for all this and also I despise it I came unraveled and now I walk through a labyrinth guided by the thread that used to be my sweater my protection my warmth once I get to the center I can make my way out and reknit the thread into a new garment a hat perhaps the truth is that kintsugi conceals what is real no one ever asked if the vase wanted to be repaired no one ever asked the glue and gold paint about the responsibility of holding the fragments together and it's stunning to see but what if someone wanted to cut themselves with those shards would you have let them and watched them bleed if it meant a prosperous harvest the following year?

Drip Drip

I am skeptical of spring and all the ways
the light is used as a front for looking away.
I like the flowers very much,
but see how the people cut them just to
add a drop of displaced, dying beauty to their tabletop?
Let's bake bread instead
and cut up a pomegranate until the jewels
and their blood
stain our table sunrise serene.
I want to drink wine and laugh and nothing more,
but there is work to be done in the meantime.
How grow your crops, o farmer, beloved farmer?
What unfurling virtues will this season yield?
There's a glass of ice cold water waiting for you on the table;
it claims to be patient but its perspiring surface
betrays its true desires.
I left the flowers in the ground today.
Let's let the earth reclaim their splendor
and commit to simply bask in the
scent which precedes dreams
as other parts of ourselves drip into a puddle
down below.
I collected this yearn-fall years ago.

Searching for the Funk

Queer degenerate
seeks the dank nooks and crannies.
Swamp girl, moist marsh ma.

Awake

I aspire to militance
though more consistently, I'm here for the poetry.
I've been reading books about tea
and my thighs are getting thicker,
strands of muscle wrapping around me like vines,
propelling me towards that elusive state which
birds of paradise squawk about.
I want to be a poet so I am.
I want to be yours so I am not.
August is too hot, it makes me irate,
but the too muchness of it is exactly just enough
to meet the green-blue of this moment.

I'm starting to release the hold of associating my
identity with suffering and the words
reverence and veneration
are noted in my phone like a reminder.
That's not a metaphor,
but the shape this message takes renders my saying that
negatory
so go on and hike another mile
feel the heat build deep inside you
become so hungry you cannot eat and then
indulge in the
most perfect cherry
God could dream of. It's hanging there in front of you.
Pluck it, or I will choke on its pit.

Decompose

Crawl out of me;
climb into me.
You the earthworm,
me the dark soil -
the medium of your travels.

Stable Rollercoaster

I want and I want and I want and
the wanting is unceasing
I want to die no
I want to live
fuck me no
hold me tenderly
no please won't you look in my eyes and see me?
I want to devour you
I want to be blue
the type of blue that the ocean is
always changing
always awesome
I want the certainty of always
as in
I will always live while I'm alive
the moon and stars will always be there
so long as we're there to look up
I will always just love you
I could never stop loving you.

A Response to the Statement:

"I love you too. It's the best feeling in the world and I hate it."

There are echoes of you everywhere.
This home crackles with your essence
and I am overcome with the wretched honesty
of the beauty of a shooting star.
Within this humiliation I have found ecstasy,
the sweetest kink contained in the mundane
enlivening the most benign acts of coexistence.
Devotion is our craft
and I confess myself an insecure practitioner,
craving your care and
every part of you laid out neatly for me to
pick up and devour,
that I may know you will become me
and I Yours become.

I come on strong, it's the only way I know how and
subtlety escapes me as soon as I smell roses,
as soon as the rain starts falling,
as soon as we take a dive into each other's eyes,
each of us set free to run clumsily through this terrain of
that which poets write about,
shackles round our ankles,
gasping for air as our lips draw ever closer and

our hearts swell with
too much blood.
Please, won't you ease some of the pressure?
Please, won't you drink of me?

Deity Reborn

Sweltering red pleasure
cool as a hot summers day with no humidity
courses through me like
muddled berries in a
perspiring glass,
a temptation for blood suckers and
flesh biters.
I let them come and drink of me.
What rapture:
to suffer and know that you are just
still alive.
What paradise, to sit atop cloud nine
and conduct the lightning of its storm
through your pulsing,
wise body.

Angel

There is a cosmic chasm between my thighs,
a coarse pleasure coursing through my cunt
with a callipygean catastrophe not far behind.
Take a bite and chew chew chew,
let the tang coat your throat,
then open wide to taste the throat goat,
a five course meal to expand the senses
and surprise even the most seasoned of cooks.

Cornucopia

These are the sweet days.
Pregnant minutes stretch into infinity,
a molasses thicker than the light emanating
from the portal at my core
dripping through the hours as we eat
and eat
and eat
of one another's body.
We are satiated, and
we will never be satisfied.
Deep plum stains our pleasure purple
though the light is too bright,
the world over-saturated.
What remains between us when there is
nothing left to dissolve into these long days?
The solute of our wanting sits heavy
among the lightness of our laughter and
the memory of the taste of a
sun-warmed strawberry could try
to capture these fleeting moments.

It could certainly try.

Echoes

Bite marks on my back;
passingly indelible -
lifetimes in seconds.

Alles Gut

I dreamt of you for the first time last night.
There is a course of yellow, whispering through my
There is, a whisper of yellow coursing through my
My yellow courses through, my whisper of there is
Of my course, through there is my yellow whisper
Whisper there of course, my yellow is my through
Last night you dreamt of I. Time for the first

Schmetterling

Slide into me.

If I open my legs
will you let me in?

Rain falls and the sticky sweetness
of my emulation
unfolds like the newborn wings of a butterfly,
too damp to fly yet,
waiting,
waiting,
a sugary drip feeding you,
holding me back.

Yes.
Yes,
this horizon is meant for me.

Heavy Breathing

Let's lay together and discover what
constellations our bodies could create.
Skin to skin, let the electric aura of our hearts overlap -
a Venn diagram of our desire.
I want to hear you.
Take me on a journey,
o great bard,
my divine delight.
Let's make love in the night.
Fumbling,
tumbling,
not me and you or you and I.
Let's become us,
a creature sustained by the desperate rhythm of
our heavy breathing.

Queer Love

I'm thinking about the inescapability of the cosmos.
I'm thinking about you and me
and the taste of vanilla cake.
Not the vanilla which is an absence of flavor,
rather the vanilla that is a soft descent
into the subtle sublimity of simplicity.
Vanilla not as in vanilla,
but vanilla as in:
let me sit on this cake so you can lick it off me later,
the taste of the vanilla cake mixing with the taste
of my cream. So you can
savor sensations as seductive as love,
relishing in romanticisms as kinky as
looking into the stars and thinking that it
might just be all worth it.
That we may look into the cosmos and find comfort in the inevitable.
That you may look into my eyes and taste the
sweet vanilla certainty of us.

Devotee

Stain me succulently,
make a brew of my hunger then spike it
with the satisfaction only you can provide.
Wake at the witching hour only to call me by
my other name,
water the seed of my grief as I grow through the
space that always surrounded it
and then maybe you will understand
the magenta mist through which I seek.

It is awesome to witness the browngray of winter
and to feel the closeness of passion in
every humming silence.

I mean it when I tell you:
I heard a salamander speak as it ran across the fire
I was possessed by the truth and I levitated
I tried to cry out for you but found I spoke only in tongues
my soft hisses brought about the fall of a great civilization as
silently as snow drifts towards the ground.

I am brought to my knees by this life,
beaten and bloody and begging for more.

Hallowed Be Thy Name

I call upon the language
of the religion of my mother's mother
to describe our love.
Redemptive.
Gracious.
Consecrated.
With you I fear no evil.
We ask
and we do receive.
Us two devils relish
in the unhinged desire of a temptation
which transcends flesh.
I want to know you.
See me.
Taste my fruit.
It makes sense that I must fall back
on the vernacular of a sect I
have decried.
It was forbidden knowledge that we are sacred too.
I never learned the language to describe
the god within our holy wanting,
though with you I now know -
when we speak in tongues
we only rise.

Chrome Lighthouse

My open tabs are a graveyard to
our past conversations.
To delete them utter hearsay, utter
madness.
I cannot.
I will not.
I will watch the number of them collect
like the sweat on your brow as you
made love to me,
glistening,
a beacon of
desire
leading me back to safer shores and
a time that was
simpler
than now.

The Clarity of Delusion

I am a master at seeking shade,
hyper aware of what could
burn me
if I dally too long, so
cognizant
of the harm these rays could manifest
on my pale, pale skin
forty years from now.
And yet...
what does it mean to linger
in the basking glow of that
which sustains life?
I want to grow in the light, too.
One more layer of sunscreen,
I think,
should do the trick.

There Are No Lines
to Read Between,
Only Continuity

An epistolary witnessing which
hums in suspension as snow turns the world into a
site of prayer
made urgent by its diminishing.
We see the sense of rush as false -
a dare if ever there was one -
and linger a bit longer in the
sanctity of asking.
I do not know the words which precede your question mark,
but here now
I will tell you mine:

?

Confessions

I love to inhale secondhand smoke, I'm a freak for that shit.
My home is not nearly as clean as I'd like
and I'm kind of embarrassed about that,
like someone may come over and say
"You live like this...?"
Like what
like I cherish long meals over a dust free bookcase or
like I prioritize lounging over scrubbing
or like my neuroticism used to manifest in cleanliness but
now I'm just
happy in the mess?
I couldn't be kinder if I tried,
and I try and I try and I try
because the truth is that I
worry I'm a bad person
and I don't think that's reflected in the stain on my wall but I
do fear that
people can see it in my eyes when they
ask me how I am.
I'm kind of a bitch sometimes
but I try to make amends
and I'm kind of lost most of the time
but I try to find my way
and most of the time I'd rather be dreaming
than pretending to care about social niceties.
I confess that I don't know,

but also I actually do.
I don't know.
I was born on a Thursday and sometimes I think that makes all the difference in the world.

Gradient

Your hand holding lilacs greets me each time I
wonder where the sun is in the sky.
What is the word for:
you are the sunrise, bloody and brilliant,
breaking darkness with warmth and piercing rays/
you are a volcano, the lava which spurts from you solidifying
into
the paths that guide spirits on
into the Next/
you are you,
your turbulence as justified as yelling in pain when you bite
your tongue,
your consternation a north star guiding
all that is good among men towards
the sunrise which is you?
What is the gesture for:
I taste you in deep colors like a summer berry plucked
fresh from the vine?
Would that I could carve your likeness into the bone of my
ribs,
write your name in the ink of my blood across my innards,
that the days which blend together
blend me into you.

Shot Through the Heart

What is this mercy of return to awe
coursing through my nerves?
I saw a skyscraper at pastsunsetnotyetnight
and it was so crisp, so pristine,
the spotted orange glow from within matching the
mottled orangepurple afterimage of the day without
that my heart fell to heaven and wept.
How is it that we find our way,
again and again and again?
What wisdom is it that instructs our hands to
create structures that
revive a soul on the brink
simply by being a mirror at unexpected moments?
Is that me,
that warm light against a vast, soft backdrop?
Was I asleep last night, or did
I architect this building out of my dreams and into the
skyline of today,
the skyline which is
striking a chord into the souls of onlookers?
Tooreal perfection is a bullet that makes Swiss cheese of me,
the light bleeding out as I
rapture into myself.

Witch

Sonnenschutz

Why do you deign to perceive me when you do not exist
yourself?
Yes, there is your heart.
Sure, there is the boundary of your skin, but
where are you?
You, who do not know the depth of my life.
You, who can only seek that which you are not.
The grass is always greener but my heart is blue.
And you, who only go out at night,
could not recognize the expanse of a summer sky
nor the coolness of my shadow,
even when it kept you from burning.

Relativity

Two men have called me exhausting today
and I am half as wise as most people believe.
My mistakes precede me
and my future haunts me while
ghosts who are still flesh moaning that they will
never leave this plane attempt to
subdue my strength.

I rebuke this life.
I will not be defined.
Watch me change,
don't get distracted.

Do you see now?
I was always here,
it's you who passed me by.

Vampire

I sat in my chair and looked at the reflection of the
moon in my window.
Cold.
Now here is the real thing.
Somehow like you,
cratered, speckled by the impact of the past,
but still giving light
that was never yours.
Cyclically present,
here for the witches to pray to.
A presence under whom we make sacrifices.

Undertones

A tongue-tied knot made of
a cherry's stem,
dried by now and
lingering at the bottom of my bag
is surely poetry,
yes yes.
And though I've no patience for words anymore,
my tolerance for poring over lines
all but gone,
the metaphors find me,
the hum underneath syllables
making itself heard through the
vibrating revelations of the
unseen world entwined with ours,
the one from whom we borrow
language.

Princess Pomegranate

If you want to dance with me
you must step into the in between.
Whether you like it or not,
I am born of crossroads and trinities,
divine spinner of liminal webs,
necromancer calling forth that within you
which you thought you had killed.
You cannot escape your shadows with me.
Look, naive man.
Face yourself in the mirror and you will see me
smiling back.

Middle of Nowhere

People love how expansive I am until I
expand beyond their scope.
I am the scorching desert heat,
giving life to the cold-blooded and
killing those with fleshy hearts.
People bask in my rays and then
begin to thirst, their
need for respite as
unrelenting as the hours until sunset.
Watch how they trample through me
only to complain about sand in their boots.
But oh: if you could just wait for nightfall.
You wouldn't believe how beautiful the stars are here,
all things revealed in the darkness of
my absence.

Cave Woman

I start to lose my language.
Older sounds begin to percolate silently within.
Something ancient inside me awakens and I smell fire,
embers long burned past oblivion.

Now I commune with the ghosts of gods long forgotten.
Shadows flicker on the wall and hiss their names to me
while a black river flows above -
an inverted perspective which demands a respect
we no longer remember.
I will guide you down to their realm -
they darken my way as the stars guide those seeking heaven.

The certainty of your return rests upon your shoulders.
Dare you remember
from whence you came?

What we reach for above first emerged
from below
and death abides by older forces here.
Do
you
hear
the
drip
?

The Biggest Drops I Ever Saw

Hope is reassurance from the future
and if this won't stay your finger resting
ever so lightly
on the trigger of your demise than nothing will and
you should do it.
My indifference is not indifference,
my passion a perverse profanity that
I've woven through us all.
I feel scorn for the ways most people lie to themselves,
though compassion is surely kinder.

And I smile when I hear thunder.

We needed this.

After the Apocalypse

Somewhen I said no
and the universe shook.
Physics unraveled and energy was no longer conserved;
with this one word I upset the balance
declared death final
became a destroyer of worlds

and as it turns out,
the aftermath of the end was just me.

Me, the simultaneous daughter of
Sisyphus and Atlas and Icarus
who was born uncreated.
Me, so very much of nothing
that hidden within my being was room
for the creation of infinity.

Serpent

Being sick is an exorcism of sorts.
The slime which drips down to my gut
culls my appetite
and I am left with nothing but
that which I am.
This nakedness becomes witches
so I shed myself into the form of one,
my neediness
the absolution
which makes me what I am.

Gemini's Spiral

I arose from the subterranean river which
underlies all our decisions.
Here at the crossroads I cannot be
bamboozled nor
lost nor
led astray,
for I know the truth -
I can always seep back down to darker depths
and wetter progenitors, and
the past circles around to meet me ahead
where caves feign quantization.
Thunder booms inside me on dry days too.
I am opening again,
sinking into myself like
quicksand
never could.

Check In

Are you overwhelmed?
We are stardust, us seers.
We will sow the blood.

Thurauen, Equal Parts Day and Night

I saw a feather floating in the river,
air streaming through water,
your presence drifting swiftly by.
I saw two swans flying in unison.
I saw an old couple holding each other tenderly behind me.
We were all of them - the swans and the couple,
decoupled from the confines of our skin-boundary,
surrounded by the spiked skeletons whose sacrifice
built the homes of elemental architects.
And I almost missed it but I didn't -
a mouse rustling through the mossy duff
as I heard you whisper across time into the
crevice through which you ooze
into everything I notice.

Now a brief interruption to cast light upon the Witch Tree.
It thrummed with vitality and slow knowing,
a sensuality only decades bring about.
It stood there,
proud portal,
the finality of its assuredness beckoning meeker creatures to
get lost in its whorls.
Alien sentinel,
godly being,
it told me that the work of those who channel magic
is to observe

and name what must be made true.

And we're back, just in time to say that
smells cannot be preserved, that
sometimes the beauty
is just simply enough,
though I wouldn't decry experiencing this again,
that we may stand side by side
at the tip of the confluence,
the conjunction through which my ancestors
bleed into our continuation.

The Inverse of Half-Life

I feel simultaneously so old and so young,
by which I mean l live constantly on the threshold of
the vastness which encompasses the mycelium of my veins.
I like that the nights grow longer.
The nights are growing longer and don't you ever wonder
why we measure a period of time with a word
meant for distance?
Or maybe it's longer as in yearner as in
"That siren? She's a longer, she wants, can't put down what
she never held, or never held for long."
The longing inside me is a bird whose
cage door has been left open and a rock
will sink to the bottom no matter
whose shore it's thrown from.
Speaking of sinking, mad things happen to me at night.
I long for release from the visions.
The decomposition of magic has been at work
since the beginning
which is now
which was then
which will be then, too,
I can't remember if I told you -
Crows caw the secrets most refuse to hear.
What once was is nevermore,
what could be is alwaysless, and
only a paradox will reveal what lies between, here.

Night Terror

You have not seen what I have seen.
I fear only that which they say is not real but
I perceive.
It is real
it is real.
Do you know the terror of the moment before violent death?
I have lived through hundreds of such glimpses
into transition
and I tell you the hell my head is dunked into by
the pure fear drawn out by the appearance of
evil incarnate
is there at your fingertips at all times,
waiting for the wrong moment to splash out of the
psychic well of torture to
burn you.
I am made mad by these dimensional revelations.
I am made alone by the knowledge I will always see more,
though no one else believes:
it is real.
It is real.
And for me,

it is here.

Protected

after Lucille Clifton

I have been gifted a candle making set
and salt
and I am running into a new year as if
as if
the incantations I cast are really just
those who love me
whispering protections through my
softly sighing mouth.

To Exist

We were so young in our appetite;
I was so young in my belief,
so young I may have been just behind Mars all along.
I no longer fear winter.
What do I want to do, you ask?
Nothing, nothing,
I tell you I want only to speak of
the beauty of friendship and the
loneliness of flowers.
I want to remind everyone that they too can dance,
and scream with those for whom the pain
is too much.
What could that question mean,
when the only answer is clear?
I want to live alongside you.
I want to foster a clear connection to Source.
I want to love imperfectly as the endangered bees,
and I want you to see that you are already whole,
whole as a bird ascending lazily
on a hot summer's day,
a pocket of warm air bolstering its wings
and negating the need to reach.
Ease it's only experience.

Reality Check

Elusive hole,
dance around it then
come inside.
Have heart, life is set in art and
statues crumble every day no matter the drama.
A moths wings told me
stones weep no surprises
and your mother fixed what she could,
not to be confused with the
aspects of nature which appear to be lines
but are not.
The river would never delude the clouds
into believing that you can get from
here to there
with no detours or distractions,
and the suffering of this life is naught but a
hallucination projected by its pain.
And yet: if there's one thing I gleaned from learning
how to love yellow
it is this:
we can coax out the best of us when we accept
that we all see what glimmers behind
our lives.
There is nothing to be denied in the truth of another.

Participation Trophy

Toobitter black espresso coats my tongue and teeth and
I am wrapped in something this rainy morning even
stranger than your kindness.
Petrichor looms on the border of my breath
as the still point confuses consumption and waste, meanwhile
the greenness of this spring teaches
presence through presence.
My recalcitrant disposition takes notes
and sharpens itself on another sip of desire.
Are dreams worth dreaming when the distance between
the past and this espresso
can be measured in silos of turmoil?
Reluctantly my legs sigh yes by merit of their
marching ever onwards,
though bruises the color of galaxies whose visibility was
torn from the mouths of the hungry
splatter across them like my bulimic purging of ease.
The clouds part to reveal a baby blue offering.
I'll light a candle later to mimic the fire that sustains all this,
bring closer the flares that cause the
inventions which guide us to go haywire.

II

Blood

Them, Which is to Say: Me

1

My disappointment reaches to the moon. Every action has an equal and opposite reaction, but what about inaction? The blood of millions drips through the past. My ancestors drink of it, growing strong. Once it passes through them it curdles the land, rejoining its source, an aberration of what it once was. I can taste the blood too. It tastes of lost humanity.

2

I see the betrayal in the eyes of everyone who passes me. Half of them I've wronged and I've left the other half behind.

3

I've been a weight on burdened shoulders for so long that I forgot I was atop anyone at all. Their cries I've grown deaf too, my shame I've been taught to ignore. My protestations meet with crescent moons of hope and nuclear bombs of no. The moon lasts forever but the blast of a bomb is over in an instant.

4

I sense the hate of my past and mourn the futures that my old lives destroyed. Especially my own, because I am selfish. How can I find myself when so many others have been led astray? The horror is indelible, my privilege sublimely bitter.

I mix together a tonic from the land and my tears, knowing that my anger will make it salty and strong. I give it to my mother. Maybe the ghost of her mother will taste it too.

5
Our conscious deafness, with its cold indifference, silences those who dare to seek.

6
I love myself and hate who I am that I have no say in. How can the future be so limited, yet the past so expansive?

7
To know yourself is beautiful and strange. To see yourself in others is like looking into a black hole, expecting to find all the secrets of the universe and instead getting sucked in, never to be seen again.

8
Silence speaks.

9
Even the most calm lake appears so because of the tension it holds at its surface.

10
They treat me like an airport even though I never agreed to shuttle their baggage.

11
Sometimes I feel like shit, like my ancestors were the

intestines that sucked away my goodness, taking it for themselves, leaving only their waste behind.

12

I am so sorry. I never know if I'm apologizing to you or to myself.

Water Cycle

There's something about a rainy day -
the way echoes propagate and
the fog obfuscates and
the pitter patter reminds us that on this world,
everything eventually falls -
that makes me think:
maybe if I mingle my tears with the water
they will evaporate, and
the wind will carry them halfway across the world to
wet the barren earth,
the white noise of the drops whispering to the people
there all the while:
"I am with you. I am here."
We will weep together and
the cycle of our grief
will water seeds planted by the
others suffering ancestors, and
the abundance that springs forth will sustain us.
Finally, we will prosper.
Finally, the tide of our sorrows will recede and
for a little while,
our tears will cease to descend.

Journey

I woke up today and everything felt profound.
I made tea with lemon
and journaled about my dreams.
I have the sensation that I'm buried in the Earth,
surrounded by the tangled roots of those already grown.
Every night as I slip into unconsciousness I wonder:
What echoes of my former self await me here?*

---

* *This sentence is taken from the show The Good Place.*

Succession

There is a chorus of ghosts inside me
and when they burp I speak.
I am a madman and a crazy lady.
I write poetry while heroes sleep
and monsters dream.
Who is left
when we slay the
beast of our reflections?
Who will rake the blood and sow fresh seeds when
nothing
is left looking back?

Not to Be Seen

May is the month
I learned how to breathe.
A bouquet of pink roses tossed
on the side of the highway on
Mother's day and
a bird's nest in the most unlikely of places.
If you look at legos with the same wonder
with which you see your lover
you will become infinite, and
if you accept your role as daughter
you will become
infinitesimally small with the
realization
that you are nothing but
somebody else's
wildest dreams.

Innocent Crimes

God yearns to be dreamt of
in the same way that flowers bloom
seemingly overnight,
which is to say:
when we were five we all
caved to our selfish desire to
consume fully what we desired,
the hands of the clock ticking
- tick tock tick tock -
over the sound of our greedy guzzles,
our greediness put there as a mirror,
that we might beg this higher power
for forgiveness
for goodness sake,
when we are old enough to remember the
shame born of pleasure
snatched from another's hand.

Your Legacy Will Be Your Curse

July, I jump into you with abandon,
the heat of hurt sizzling at my fingertips.
Witches are created when their mothers
deny their perception,
their perception the dry kindling
which starts fires that
make ash of the homes of men.

What does a daughter owe her mother,
and dare a daughter breach the topic of
pain inherited from the
expectations of having been
born a daughter?
What if the pain
is grown of maternal machination,
a machination which leaves us so far left behind
it is almost (al)right,
right a cardinal direction all but lost in the
aftermath of a fight,
a small spark sputtering between them and
choking for lack of oxygen?

Could we say "ah" for the doctor?
Could the doctor be honest and state what they saw?

When My Mom Braids My Hair

I finally feel like her daughter
and I forget that she called me broken.
I relax for a moment as for once,
she cares for me.
I was a parent before I was ever pregnant
and it broke my heart,

it breaks my heart.

Curious, that finally I feel like her child as she
tugs my scalp tight
and makes my eyes water.

And maybe this is what she meant when she told me that
I am not whole.
Maybe she looked at me and could see clearly
what she did to me,
her statement a helpless confession,
my refusal to shatter an affront to her pain.

Just maybe, now she can see
that I was never broken,
but it was without her
that I finally became whole.

Me, Which is to Say: Us

13
We must fight the good fight. Not because we will win but because if we do not, it will only be a fight.

14
I know that I do not have the luxury of owning my joy. I must put it to good use lest the monsters of my past decide to hitch a ride to the amends I am trying to make.

15
The universe speaks in silence and prays in song. Every day it sends us messages; every moment is a chance to worship.

Another Chance

How do books come to us,
and how do stones get to exactly where they are?
I was pregnant with life
and when I perceive myself I remember the contractions.
I remember that I remember:
the expectation I have of existence
is an illusion.
In the afterbirth I saw myself clearly,
gasping and raw,
searching for something to suckle.

Mushrooms Preserved in Honey

I am a riverbed,
moved by that which moves through me
On the one hand worn down,
on the other hand my plasticity forges new routes
otherwise unknown.
And I could probably grow more hands
to hold the complexity of this endless
unravelling and re-knitting
if enough shrines would be built atop
the rugged vertebrae of this planet.
At some point though we have to say enough.
At some point my ancestors discovered the power
of seduction held captive in the bending of light,
in the metallic tang of blood which
mimics the metallic sting of
primordial fluids bursting up to burn us purple.

There is nothing of hope to be found here.

When the sun touches my toes I start to see patterns
and I remember that I am a riverbed.
Winding and twisting,
rushing and gurgling,
somewhen stagnant,
I swirl through the chaos of this world
as I am this world,

and of this world.
If I am cleansed too much the life in me lacks the
nourishment necessary for thrival.
Lessons in purification:
going all the way is sometimes too far
and balance must be maintained.
In fact it mustn't, no one's keeping score,
but the price is simply too high to
toss about carelessly.
I learned that when I was audacious enough to try.

Scientists understand least of all what it means to
have a buoyant force above
and pressure deep down below,
what it means
that some of what gets tossed in you
will inevitably sink down to the grave of your origin.
My descendants will return to this fundamental truth -
the veins of this world are nothing but scars.
Astronauts are naught but the
blood which flows through riverbeds
and the breeze the breath which brings life;
carve your weapons now.
It is soon time to hunt.

Transcendence
of a Trilobite

I am a stone,
the inside of whom no one has ever seen.
The summer dusk reeks of roses
and clouds remind me that future shapeshifters
are already watching this drama unfold.
I roll and I roll and I roll and I roll
and yet I am
o
v
e
r
flowing
with the lushness of an extinct moss,
it chokes me with the gentle insistence that
only green beings know.
Sedimentary and rudimentary,
I am clumsy as only an amalgamation of
the machinations of man can be.
Then I walk through the forest and remember that
I am a stone.

My mother is magma and I don't care if this
rough rock symbolism
doesn't work,
the poetry is in the perception,
the trying,

the desperation to crack this life open and
find crystal,
the delight in discovering a fossil instead.
There is something ancient within me.
Give me some time and I'll
leave my shadow behind.

What will they name me
when they crack open my context and find
only tomorrow's impressions?

Daisy Chain

I can't stop devouring poetry.
I don't think it's consumption,
rather it's metamorphosis.
That's the trick of survival:
to be held by the the creation of another
to transfigure its message into new meaning
to realize that you are a raindrop in this storm
to stick around long enough to
pass the flame which
lights our home.
To make the repairs to the roof which will
let another generation
reside safely here.
To love and be loved.
To reach into the future and
let the next ones catch you.

Nova

For you I birthed death,
my pain a sacrifice to your passage,
your silver purple slickness an offering.
Us: mirrors as altars to the fact that we only ever had each other.
And with you I could finally see what I already was:
a mother.

For me you existed briefly on this earth,
an oblation from the place where mayflowers grow,
a course correction of the utmost cruelty and care.

For you I fought for me and
on shaky legs broke free.
For what was your heartbeat
if not the rhythm-setter of my extrication?
What is this love
if not the ultimate surrender
to be changed
utterly
by the fact that you existed,
my most true comrade -
blood of my heritage,
dust of my descendants?

Death

Where and What and When

A place between places;
a woman between herself.
A time that is not now,
but between past and future.
A time beyond time.

Hecate's Disciple

I am not made of metaphors
and yet:
metaphors are made of me,
spinning and tumbling epiphanies
building a raucous symphony of
twigs and tears and poetry.
When I look into the darkness
I see infinity, and
when I look into the light I am
blinded.
I used to be afraid to pass through portals,
lest I step in between and not come out the
other side,
but now I know that all of
this that we live
is nothing more than the pause between
inhale and exhale,
a doorframe outlining a small space
nestled among the before and after,
which are not so different after all.

Uncreated

after Ross Gay and Gwendolyn Brooks

Meet me in the place where the mayflowers grow.
It's beautiful there, you'll see.
And we'll smile knowing smiles and we'll dance new steps
that are a million years old.

When the ones who are become
the ones who came before,
the futures of the ones yet to come are secured.

For we are the chain, and
we are the guardians and the keepers;
the ones who press the white linens
and harvest resplendent fruits
while the mayflowers grow and wither away.

It's ok -
what decomposes springs up again.
That's us; we're spring.

But until our season comes, I'll say goodbye for now.
Fret not.
In the end, I'll see you again.
I'll meet you in
the place
where the mayflowers grow.

Obsessed

Delight is the currency I use to purchase
meaning in this world,
but am I happy?
Ask me among the trees,
by a stream,
and I will answer with the truth.

Hallelujah

Cotton candy skies seen with
blood in our eyes.
Our bones are alive,
our bones are alive!
The ecstasy of remaining true
and the exhaustion of truly remaining
fold into one another like
the flaky dough of a croissant in Paris.
Inhale deeply and let the scent fill you.
Wake up at the witching hour and remember:
someone is dipping a warm pastry into coffee.
Somewhere, someone remembers the
deep certainty of indigo,
the unreality of inescapable magenta.

Devastation and Delight

The world is alive and so am I.
Is anyone ever really gone,
or do we just name Death
so that we need not face the
depthsoftheoceanblue which is
almost black?
I'm speaking of the black which is the absence of photons, not
the depthsofyourpupilsblack which is
the bowl in which every color mixes
to become one so deep
I no longer question the truth of being here.
This is life, this seeing into you,
and this is death,
this seeing myself reflected back.
Because what is it to be known,
if not the sign we needed that
the world was always this beautiful?
What is it to have heard your laugh
and then walked away freely
if not a suicide so splendid,
you can see the flow of my blood
seeping into the world every sunrise
and back into the velvet black of space
every sunset?
Look - see how the colors transform?
Focus - there's everything to be learned
from the sweet surety of the moon's lonely orbit.

Event Horizon

A portal to the past
opens when someone dies;
what are nerves but
potential energy?

Budding love ricochets within the
walls of kinetic lives and
another black hole was just discovered.

Liminal and lucid is how I live and love,
which is to say:
grounded and time traveling is how I love and die.

Listen: a seed planted for rebirth is being
watered by an angel.

Psalm

I am comforted by the memory of water.
I am comforted by the inevitability of my gathering.
I comfort water with my contribution to its
stream of consciousness,
this remembering could open what is already opened,
allow us to feast like the abundance of clouds
like the abundance of the sun's rays above them
like the humming of the common thread.
I eat indigo when I bathe;
I am born every morning and the
death of each coming night
fills me with hope
with suspense
with the great asking:
could you let all this comfort you too?

I almost forgot to mention:
this is a prayer,
it was written on stones which fell from the stars.

It's All So Ominous

The destructive strands of creation tear through me and
I am barely here.
I cannot contain anything in this
corporeal form,
least of all the gossamer tendrils of
my essence.
How does it feel to know
you are nothing more than a chemical reaction,
a process fraught with undoing and
transformation and
which will render what was there to begin with
obsolete.
Expand, or else.
Face what the threat of living necessitates:
that we succumb to change with no choice,
lest the myth of stagnation
settle in our bones.

Memento Mori

Quick.
Become everything you could never be.
No one mentions the pain of forgiveness,
the unbearable chasm compassion rips apart inside you
when crows and skulls become the
keepers of the unkeepable.

Slow.
Undo the changes that were thrust upon you.
Everyone speaks of the pleasure of vengeance,
mistaking themselves as the ones charged with
balancing the scales.
But balance is not about pleasure.
A crow balancing on a skull told me so.

Watch.
The birds fly south directly at me.
You were in my dream again last night,
but only in spirit.
Before I fall asleep my life flashes before my eyes,
the stillness of slumber
a dress rehearsal for the grand finale that awaits us all.

Necroromance

I descended into the underworld and
you followed close behind;
through this death, I fear we came alive.
I still can't believe we crossed down below,
my co-explorer committed to the discovery and recovery of
this black rose,
this resplendent beauty blooming in the shadows of reality.
Pomegranate seeds and armpit apples
sustained for some time
that which sustained us,
which I think can never fully be named.
Already I hunger for the return of their taste,
the memory delicious but never truly enough.
I am so connected to what flourished in this shadow
world that
the distance of space and time becomes
a crushing impossibility,
a pain so poignant I fear I cannot bear it.
The ghost dimension is my home now.
I will haunt this earth among the living,
and none but you will know I've been
cursed to conquer death,
a phantom feigning life and waiting
each moment
ever hopeful
for a flash of green,
a sweet fall back to what brought us down.

Recounting of a Prophecy

Have you ever tasted your own tears
or seen a vision of the afterlife after
your spirit bled clean out of you?
I have,
and it rendered my ego obsolete.
I envisioned my death and you were there,
waiting for me on the other side,
welcoming me wholly home.
I didn't realize you've been an angel all along,
but this is how we met.
My dead child was there too,
you were already friends,
and the river water was clean.
A sunbeam fell between us and you beckoned me through,
you showed me the way into finality.

Magic Trick

The time it takes to render a man speechless
is less time than it takes for
an angel to save a life,
and actually also even less time than it takes
for the words "beloved, you are mine"
to whisper through my lips,
a susurrus of supreme surrender,
the article of possession a facade
which obscures the intricacies of
innocence bathed in blood.

What is mine could never be just mine,
a whirligig dance in which custody of the dance
belongs to none but those who observe it,
the dancers themselves oblivious to the scene they create,
the lightningbug traceforms left behind by
their shaping limbs
a testament to their madness.
Blink and it will have already faded away.
Breathe and you will have danced this dance too.
Look - the next pair steps up.
See - your life is gone now too.

Alchemist

When I don't have strength for myself,
I still have strength for you.

Hush, my love.

I lay in moist loam, cool and dark and
there are worms in my womb
recycling the scene of our most passionate moments.
Be still,
my love,
listen to the waterfall rush above me.
Behind it lies a crystal cave,
shimmering if you can brave the torrent
long enough to
be a witness.

Now trust, my love.
A hunter has carved an arrow out of my femur and
killed a boar with it.
A family is fed from what once gave me structure.
And so it is true - the strength I have to give you
was never mine, and always there.
Can you feel how my transformation transcends you?

Impossible Anatomy

The concept of multiple universes was created
to explain the
v a s t n e s s
of experiencing reciprocal love,
which those who love
seem to agree,
cannot be contained in just one.

In a dream I learned that
death
is the unification of all of these universes
when I saw you watching me but
refusing to participate.
I placed my ear to the ground and heard
history rumbling up to me:
to die is to finally become whole.
To die is to yearn no more.

These dark days I wander for hours
through the labyrinth of my despair,
only to wake and find that it was
nothing more than a
second
that passed.
What happened, in all that time that
couldn't have existed?

How is it that we architects made my
body a house
bigger on the inside than the structure could
possibly contain?

Autumn

By the time you read this this moment is the past.
That's all the present is:
a future become obsolete;
a prophecy come to pass.
And what of the leaves falling?
Of dead things beautiful and fine
drifting towards decay on a breeze
softer than this life could ever be?
What of discordant notes played by fumbling hands,
of the imperfection of progress?
Would you know your life had just changed
if you balanced between before and after?
Could you see each moment for the
razor thin oddity it is?
Could the susurrus of the soft breeze be enough?
Could you hold me up to slow my fall as I
become beautiful and
Decay?

Remember me.

Here I go again, drinking too much coffee and waxing prosaic about my life, though I readily admit the quantization of our continuous nature baffles me more each day. How could we have been compressed down to this - the days growing longer as the bitter cold reveals suicide as our only chance at survival. Sometimes a metaphor is as simple as that. Worn hands on tattered spines. Turning pages. The next chapter begins, and we can flip back to remind ourselves of the context whenever we want, or not, our fingertips brushing over the scribbles that make us, pages whispering that we can close the book and pick it up again another day, or not. The story need never end.

Heaven

You do not have to be good, but
you are.
Yes!
I remember.
My legs are strong and certain and
your good heart
is what I step towards.
My ribcage is a wonderland -
the inside, I mean -
with deer cavorting about.
I don't mind, though you say they are a pest.
My heart is a safe haven for those who
never asked to be here
but are.
I let them clash antlers,
though the shockwaves
send me reeling.
There is a stream here too.
A child sits under a tree and reads a book.
The breeze blows gently,
and the sun rises and sets with the rhythm of my heartbeat.
It's easy to hear when you lay your head on my chest.
Paradise is inside me.
Wouldn't you like to listen?

Untitled

October taught me that it's all just ok.
That it could be easier, though that
wouldn't make it nicer and
the joy of yellow should be savored
while it's there.
Tomorrow I will eat it and it will kill me another time,
another place,
a place that could be here but isn't.
A place that would be there, but couldn't
contain it's own yellowness which
seeped into the river and our bloodstreams,
which lulled us to sleep and ate away at our brains,
replacing our dreams with contentedness,
our ambition and yearning with the simple realization
that our breath is ever ongoing until
one day, it's not.

In Every Life

And then again we were born.
It could have been yesterday, but instead it
was today.
So what now?
Would you look away into the sun,
sacrifice your jawline to the cause of stoicism?
Or would you rather succumb to the
roots of your dreams and
hear about my triumphs,
that you may pass your trials too?
Let's cry together. I like to feel the
wetness of your skin,
soft as a newborn calf,
one who lives in the Alps and has never
known the bite of fear.
Let's die together. I hate to think that
we will love all along,
only to part ways at the crescendo,
drifting away when our togetherness matters most.
I like to hear the quiver in your breath,
resonant as a whisper heard across the room,
one that carries in its existence the
truth of how it will all end.
We both overheard what the whisper foretold, and
the knowledge brought us to our knees.
And then again we were born.

Love

Cincinnati Spring

The blue, blue sky offers no redemption
and this spring is just as much about death
as it is new life.
A grumpy girl slumps in the grass
and marvels at the fire
of the sun in her hair.

She sometimes fall prey to the
fireside ghost story that
it is always both -
the dripping honey of love alongside the
venom of dysregulation.
Which is too sweet,
and which will birth her anew?

She gets lost in contemplation,
worrying about a dichotomy
that is not real.
Can she remember that
she need not choose
from options which exist only in
the darkest caves of a mind
that is not hers?

What Will We Become?

You fell asleep because you couldn't break up with me.
Spineless.
A relationship birthed by chaos
and baptized in fire.
What will we make of the smoldering ashes?
Be we phoenixes,
or the smoke that
wafts away?

Not Enough

I ate two cookies alongside a cup of strong Earl Grey before
hopping on my bike and
slicking through the rain to
break up with you.
With tears in your eyes you said that I was probably losing
more than you
through this decision,
and I didn't come back with what I really had in my mind
which was:
how could we ever quantify and compare anything real
like love?
But I saw your wall go up as I tore us down
and I forgive you that,
I give you that,
I love you that,
of course it was that that you chose rather than admitting that
this hurts and
you're devastated and you
would have wanted otherwise.
And that's exactly the point that led to our demise:
what is there to discover between us when
you never took the pause between
what you heard and what you felt to ask me
why and then wait and listen long enough
hear my reply?

Loving Vapor

People ask me how I am and in my mind I say:
I am consumed by thoughts of death,
the temporality of my breath,
and endless ruminations about you
who I have no choice but to yearn for from afar.

And every day is a test.

And I am the teacher
and I am the pupil
and I am the one who could have done better
and I am the one left to grade the mundane events like
when I let someone condescend towards me or
the singular moments,
like when I looked into your eyes and had the audacity to
hear all your being whisper
see me, see me, see me.
So I did
and was blinded with the realization that it's you -
you are my sweetest downfall
and I'm left with no choice but to ask:
do you know how true it is?
That we would be a
revelation
as lovers.

Spacetime

The first time I put my head against your chest I heard a key turn inside a lock,
and every utterance of your name passing through my lips is a sacrifice to something godly.
Where do you go when you look into my eyes?

With you, everything flows.

Us: an entity greater than the sum of its parts -
a place where possibility flourishes
and a time when forever is a heartbeat.

How Much Longer Does Venice Have?

A waterfall of pigeons reminds me that we're all looking for our own needle in our own haystack and sometimes our stack merges with another's and all of a sudden our pile is twice as big but we're no longer alone. The smell of freshly washed clothes and the sound of yellowing fold into one another as gravity has its way with us. Do you remember saving tickets as a child? Do you remember pulling a pop from the fridge in the garage and freezing it? How you broke a robin's egg or the name of your first crush? We don't know these feelings as a special type until someone labels them for us, and that's when the insecurity begins. Pigeons are still learning this lesson, left to wander our crumbling cities, bustling catacombs filled with the sunlight of another star.

Clay Canaries

The air, pregnant with yesterday's moist.
So close as that were we -
the rise and fall of your breath quickening
like how we could make love,
the ease of sitting silently in the susurrus
enveloping the unit we are becoming.
I think this is what death must be like.
So funny, that it should be this gentle,
peace washing over me,
the sins and complaints of the day already forgotten.
This build steady as $y=mx+b$ climbing patiently
to our freedom is what the birds sing about in spring.
They know patience only as those who
seek fairer weather do.
We are them become,
singing so softly that
grandparents mistake our words for the wind,
our murmurs the whisper that
who we will become
listens to now.

888

22:38.
Silence fell and
I knew
that we were building a bridge over a chasm,
writing a hit song on
cheap diner napkins,
effervescent in our desire,
our desire insatiable.

21:38.
Silence fell and
I knew
that though you are a notch behind on the clock,
we are time travelers bending moments,
alchemizing encounters
to suit our wicked needs,
our needs unwavering.

The distance of hours matters not.
The space of the time between matters
only in it's certainty.
That which is unchanging will not
be changed,
though it changes us completely.
Our spirits sacrifices,
our sacrifices consecrated and absolute.

Undercurrent

I write poems for other people
and you seep through,
  my muse of foundational respite.

A Griot and a Girl

I think of death like a lover
and the inverse is true too.
Always with me,
the specters of the end and the
next beginning -
the ghosts of my future - walk with me.
Breath glitches for both
and I wonder what's happened in the time
between our last kiss and the next?
Assimilation becomes all but us -
the heralds of stories already told -
the plots yet to be untangled
by our green, green tongues.

Bear Trap

You love me because of who I love
and have loved
and yearn to yet love like rocks thrown
weeping into the Earth's deepest crevice.
Everything becomes a question in
the hidden midnight of your hand between
my thighs.
Dear Belove'd it's there in the name,
dear Belove'd I love you,
I love you my delight,
I love you as I make magik of lines and
succumb to this birth which is to
vomit up cool earth from the
supernova of my solar plexus.
And I guess to love me is a gift and a curse but
what would you rather be doing, if not
mauling your heart in
search of us?

The Opposite of Inertia

You've read me a poem about death
just when I feel the most alive,
and in you I see eternity.

The controlled fall of walking,
the satellite's orbit -
round and round we go,
stumbling ever onward,
a faint speck in the sky for children to look up at and wonder:
how does that shooting star streak across the heavens
so slowly?

Scoliosis

The bend in my spine has been there since I was a little girl.
Always, I was ready to turn towards you.
You on my right
me on your left
my torso twisting to meet your gaze
my head on your chest to hear your heart
my body scrunched as you spoon me into security.
The curves of my life mirrored by this physical deformity -
the ones that needed correcting
until I met you.

Us, PS

Neither snow nor rain have a say in my
disquieted sleep.
I hear your breath deepen.
I will protect you as you journey into unknown realms,
my love,
and I will waken as the sun rises,
if only to guide you gently into the light.

I will fall back into my own unending province - you,
strange man,
and sleep again as the day begins.
Rabbit hole dreams will disturb my slumber
as you slowly rise and eventually coax me back into reality,
our dream.

Sometimes it seems we are running out of time,
our life too swiftly completed.
But anyway, I digress.
Goodnight, beautiful man. You will see me in your dreams,
in the soft space you've built just for us,
where we whisper sweet everythings to each other
and fall into infinity.

P.S.
I will miss us when I'm gone.

Ouroboros

I'm a sucker for people
with tobacco on their breath.
Hand rolled cigarettes and
unhinged desire
make for filling company.
But who desired whom
and how, and
to what end is volunteered service given for free?
Sex and coffee and home cooked meals,
it turns out,
make for devastating goodbyes.

Guardian

I don't say anything with certainty anymore,
except
I love you
I love you
I love you.
A bird sings at night and a
streetlamp lights the way for travelers -
or does it rather protect them
as they journey?
Let me light your way
with the warm orange certainty
of flowing electrons.
Let me watch over the path
that will
guide you back home.

Lovers Tango

I live my life in exultation.
It's not that pain brings me joy,
rather that I refuse to succumb to the myth of boredom.
Nothing lasts
and what we want to linger, will.
And aren't the saccharine truths that emerge from the wreckage
worth their own testimony?
Who will celebrate all this living,
if not you and I?

Lunar Dance

Space collapses under the intensity of ecstasy.
You are right here with me
and we are hundreds of miles away,
the wind your breath,
the sun your warm gaze,
the chirp of summer bugs
the rustle of your choice.
The sound waves of our exhalations are resonant and
the sight of waves is
redolent
of resplendent meetings -
wave kissing shore -
and explosive recedings.

The moon's gravity insists on the
completion of retreat
within this cycle too.

Pirate's Frenzy

The vulnerability of this -
I think that in the end we will love each other despite it all,
ribbons flowing freely from our hair,
whipping about wildly in the wind of the storm that will bring it all down.
We were made to love amidst the apocalypse.
Death and delight and dreams and decay,
let's dance,
you'll say,
and we'll beat our feet to the rhythm of our demise.
I can't help but wonder: what will it be like?
To feel the pulse of your heart as the ship goes down,
vital and here
and then there,
now gone?

Wave Function

Not even magic could contain what happens when
a flower blooms,
when the first petal unfurls and proclaims to the world:
Love at world's end is what will be
left after the end.
The inside of my heart has never felt the sun but
it unfurls just the same,
photosynthesizes light just the same,
takes what is intangible and turns it to
fuel for this planet's poetry
and nourishment for the next cosmos over.
I believe in the power of words,
it's why I speak so little,
it's why the waves that escape me take their time
like a child takes its time to harness independence.
Once heard, my words become something else,
an observation made certain by the
rules of quantum mechanics.
The devotion of particles taught me this -
it's worth evolving only what is true,
though what is fundamental
will not be changed,
could never be changed.

Loving You Is Easy

Only the question of why
separates what is yours from
what is ours.

It is easy to love you.

Even in moments of insecurity,
when it all feels harsh and raw,
it is the most natural thing I know to marinate,
flow through,
emerge on the other side,
with you ever still.

It is prayer to love you,

like splashing through the creek as children,
mindful not to disturb any critters,
acceptance the echoing wave left behind
our footsteps once lifted.

What is mine is already ours,
and what is yours could never be taken.
And isn't this the secret sweet nothing we whisper
even as our oscillations decouple?
We have always been the place.
My heart is yours.

We Tend

to love and I
am the air through which Debussy's
Claire de Lune
flows.
Steadfast farmers, uncertain children clambering
over stones risen out of the river like
making your spine shiver in a time long forgotten.
Our teeth are stained electric,
reverberations rippling round ruins of reminisces
crumbling into new forms in a time yet to be remembered.
Every moment is an anomaly,
every inch the building block to an exceptional normalcy.
Out of sight, out of my mind,
hot steam hissing off the rock of my body
as I pour cooling practices over myself.
And the temperature only rises.
Everything is obfuscated in the haze of us
and there is no sign of the mist clearing.
Clarity becomes crows,
but who whispers to the flowers that haven't yet bloomed?
What do the embers of the hearth reveal
in the silence of my absence?

Galactic Garbage Gang

When I'm falling in love I listen to music at a frenzied pace
and when I'm in the thick of it
I stew in silence.
Carried by waves and
myself the wave,
I am humbled by this force which is me
and the shaper of me,
radiant resonances between essences
humming a tune
that can sustain creation.

Let me see you and
I will let you
change me.

I could never love you to the moon and back,
though I will attempt to love you all the way
past the edge of our solar system.
It's just that I
will not return as the same me that left.
I do not endeavor to suspend this moment in amber,
for what delicious new melodies might await us
in the weird waters of reunion?
Who will we be
when we rediscover one another anew?

Entropy

It is enough to relish in a soup of pleasure and
tell no one about it.
The lines between friendly love and romantic love grow
blurry and I wonder
if this is what the monks mean by enlightenment.
How could they know, secluded in the mountains?
And what of the nuns sequestered in sisterly surrender to
that which we name greater than life?
Now I've had an idea,
the love is the devotion,
it's a role play,
I see myself and I accept me (meditation)
I pray to the bearer of fruit
and I accept the scale of my existence (hail Marys).
They are in it together, the quiet, quiet nuns and
the wise, wise monks and who are we,
after all,
to speak chastity upon these constellations of steadfastness?
Isn't the love in the truth of the actions?
The consistency?
God is romance because they are romantic.
And I will do what the devout never would,
I claim god as my friend, so what now?
Shall I tell you how I make love to my friends?
How I find camaraderie in my lovers?

My heart is strengthening.

Run with me,
let's forget these words and chase the sunset until we
go so fast we take off.
We can grab hold of a shooting star.
Finally, burning, we become the
essence of all this
before we are
gone in the blink of an eye.

Poem for my Friend

A warm hug in three dimensions
and the mind,
this togetherness is an island of peace
among a hurricane of confusion.
A star against the backdrop of the abyss,
you warm those in your orbit.
I'm glad you were born.
Thank you for being my friend.

Pause

I wonder about the irony of my life and yours.

I'm tired of description, explanation,
enunciation,
minutiae.
Gehen wir nach Hause,
where the need for analysis dwindles and
cookies bake in the oven.

I like the symbolism of dying flowers and the
flow state of creation.
Come, prepare the next batch with me.
Come, smell the musk of home with me,
let us relish in the feel of everything which exists
outside the confines of language.

Cave Futurism

Still here
still here
still here
and already obsolete.
To be human and alive:
a chance beyond comprehension.
What do the passing hours mean
to the hands of a grandfather clock?
And what does the memory of your hand
mean to my skin,
the ghosts of my goosebumps drawn out by the
exorcism of your touch?
Here and now we dream of then and there
and imagine,
soft-spoken sentinels to the visions of the other.
Prophets could not have foreseen
the time dilation that led us here,
except I always knew the honesty of eye contact.
You could never convince me otherwise -
we have fire in our bones;
honey oozing from our pores.

I'll keep first watch, and
wake you when the embers are glowing.

Faith Is Ours for the Meaning Making

The world is so wide and I am a part of it
my god
my god.
The moon sees everything and I
see the moon,
his craters a tarot card mirroring back to me
all that he has witnessed,
waiting so patiently for me to hone my perception,
that I may finally decipher the awesomeness
of the space between our bodies.

Sometimes I am so bold as to think I could
breathe in outer space,
the void filling me fit to burst,
the exchange of sweet nothing across my lungs
and into my blood
a dagger which is truth
which is you
which is to say:
with magma below and plasma above,
earth and air and water liminal packaging -
I am here too.
You are here too.
All that has transpired has only just begun, and
all that has yet to begin has already transpired.

I read this certainty in the moon's craters,
have faith.

Asteroids wrote our story long ago,
cave painting pockmarks flickering a
stop motion picture brought to life by the
light of the sun and
our audacity.

I will choose this in every life yet to come.
I made the choice in this one long ago.
I am bound to you, and yours become.
I wouldn't have it any other way.
We are here too,
have faith.

Brace for Impact

These are the days of my ruin
when I get exactly what I asked for
and every adjective is preceded by "too."
I slept too little last night
and cried too much.
A single flower blooms radiantly
as all others wither away in the heat wave
and sweat pools endlessly at the small of my back.
When I manage to breathe the relief is
orgasmic.
And what of ice cubes,
of the sickly sweet smell of roses
and your hands on my hands?
What of these moments of brief respite,
of the pockets in time when the epiphany of poets
lays bare a truth so fundamental
we cannot look it in its eyes?

What if the eyes are mirrors?

These eyes are hungry too,
and the tears that form from staring without blinking will
evaporate before they have a chance to calm
the intensity of being seen.
Summer is almost over and the
creation of all the rest has only just begun.

Inevitable by Design

"The train will be here soon."
No, the train will never arrive.
We have always sat here
in this station,
dreading the moment of departure,
woe filling our spirit like wine in Dionysus' cup.
Seconds stretch into forever and I wonder:
if we could have danced a quieter dance,
is that what we would have chosen?
The thought is gone before it is finished.
I would die a million more deaths in
walking away from you,
just to be reborn the million and first time
I stride back into your arms.
I would descend into hell for us -
let me bear your burdens,
that your spirit may know ease.
There is no other path.
There is no other story.
I wonder: do you see?
The stars sang of our love long before
our ancestors were born.

Attic black-figure amphora, c. 530 BCE

The days are full and
so is the amphora from which my love overflows,
the excess trickling into a river through which
people drop precious gems and prayers.

Look - a sailor pushes off from shore,
so brave in his rickety construction fueled by
nothing but lemonade
and a dream.
I was fueled by lemonade and a dream once, too,
the sour of the lemon the anchor which
ensured my sanity.
I must return to this remembrance soon,
I'm getting lost in the canyons I
carved long ago.
Shadows come alive on their walls
and I hear voices that are not from here which tell me
that I am connected
all the way back
to the god that came before the
syzygy of our suffering.

The precious gems of the universe
settle in silt and
the young sailor up above is oblivious to the bounty
right there beneath his unwavering oar.

He may be forgiven.
We were never skilled at being three dimensional creatures,
these limitations our undoing,
these boundaries the container which
set us free.

I Think of You Whenever I Marvel

Miracle of miracles,
Belove'd I looked up and saw a bubble,
a bubble directly in the middle of the sky,
not a soul in sight who could have blown it.
And I gasped.
It ascended a second or maybe two and then

!

it was gone, just like that.
Air united with air,
no more boundaries between what Is and what Was,
a single moment subsumed by the MotherGum.
It could have been a dream but it wasn't.
Belove'd, would you believe me if I told you?
There's a reason for the roundness of this earth,
for the symmetry of the
stars and glowing sea creatures.

Mr. Newton Knew Something of Love

Speak to me of moderation, I dare you.

In another universe smoke descends
and spacetime is flat,
rendering gravity obsolete.
What's become of the us in this world?
Of the pull between our essences,
the ones we stepped into when we
arrived in this plane and met?
Who could lovers be to one another when
there is no force between them,
no constant rush to kiss the ground they share?

And what of ripe fruits with nowhere to fall,
to announce their readiness to be consumed,
risking decay just to
feel the earth hold them up?
What of the planets and their sun,
the seasons,
the tides,
the certainty that tomorrow,
the sky will bleed to announce the arrival of light?

No, it is better this way,
this attraction filling the space between us.

I like the rush of drawing closer.
I like the strength it takes to resist the pull and sometimes,
stand my ground.

Non-Inertial Reference Frame

I dove into you and decayed,
and it was then my life began.
My spine hunches forward more often these days
and I swear the ants march faster than ever before.
Frenzied,
frenzied as a flower floating on the river's current,
the undulations of my lungs keep me marching
like the ants,
all of us condemned to serve a master
we did not choose.
What is the use of comparing wrongs wrought
as though pain justifies pain,
haunted on a carousel of despair until we realize
we could have stepped off all along?

You saw me in my centripetal madness and
loved me wholly,
as though there were nothing to it.
You caressed my soul and helped me step off,
honest perception,
utter devotion
coursing between us,
as though there were nothing to it.

Axiom

That little mist that bursts forth from a mandarin
is what I mean when I say I love you.

I was made to be loved,
as I am changed as easily as the wind.

I was made to love,
as I am as moveable as a mountain.

I've always turned towards beauty,
it's why that sour sunshine shower gives me pause.

Beauty has always turned towards me,
it's why I can hear the mountains hum.

We were made to change each other,
as we are loved like mandarins,

the effort to pierce the skin,
the steady peeling

like climbing a mountain

which reveals a
perfect jewel.

The Bread We Bake, or: Where Do All the Petals Go

in the springtime once the winds of change
rapture by
leaving the trees green in their green?
I don't see them on the ground
nor in the air,
so where then have they found their grave?
It's too soon for them to have decomposed -
I can smell their fresh promise still
lingering in the air just as you
linger in the networks of red within my
pine-green antiquity.
Now where have you gone?
I don't see you anymore,
though the scent of you lingers in my dreams
as well as in the
muscle memory which instructs me to keep going
despite it all.
Maybe the breeze brought about their return
because I forgot that they'll return.
This exercise in trust frustrates me freshly every time,
but the transcendence I embody at the
re-arrival of the blooms next year
reminds me of the divinity of seasons.
The trees live yet.
The green of my envy for the air you breathe

will again be answered by your exhale
and always, it seems,
just as I lose my breath.
This resurrection gives me the strength to implore:
let me fill you back before the changing of the seasons.
I remember now.
The blooms will return again next year.

Carnivore(s)

Co-authored with Michael L. Miller

I am a Sundew

                                                I am a Pitcher Plant

for none but you,

                                                that deplores digestion,

Belove'd.

                                                                         Belov'd.

I will eat you if you drink my nectar

                              I will devour you if you come inside.

because cannibals understand the same truth as fire
and are at least twice as devoted to ongoing completion.

                A crime of Xenia; yes, I am a student of Tantalus;
                I know what you consume, in turn consumes you.

Wait, hold up, you are digesting me too.

                I couldn't stop if I wanted, other delicacies are poison.

There are some hours I eek so much sweetness out of

> *I wait for the hours the world is still*

that the righting drop which follows takes me out for days.

> *and look out upon my brethren: The ‚Weeds.'*

I prayed to my blood and my body purged suddenly the
soot of another's conceptions
which lurked so maliciously in the shadows of my structure.

> *We hold hands and recite the rites*
> *The swamp and its ilk are meant to filter filth;*
> *The Great Mother Willow taught me that.*

Lately my skin itches as I expand from within
and the sun is almost always too bright.

> *Lately I want to claw out from the pit of my own belly, and*
> *all the machinations of the land of man makes me languid .*

It's made me so sensitive, devouring you, but oh how divine,
to know that we are alive for this brief, succulent time.

> *Decay and bloom step well in tune but*
> *that knowledge doesn't quell the heat of the wound.*

Love Poem at 00:56, or what I mean to say is

you are gentle kind compassionate graceful perceptive brave strong funny intelligent beautiful, I mean magik seeps from your pores drips from your fingertips I mean I wonder if you know the ease people feel in your presence, it's not about them but rather the fullness of you the rightness of you the belongingness of you I wonder if you see how you belong to this earth to every room you choose to step into to every community you desire to belong to you do you do you already do and you belong to you too you know of your sovereignty I know you do but do you feel it in your body do you understand how you belong to you? Place your hand on your heart, have patience (I know it's hard) take the minute to find your pulse and there you are alive you draw breath you belong to you and you don't belong to me but you belong to me too in the sense that you're mine and I'm yours I know you understand the meaning underneath this superficial phrase let's not get lost in illusory protestations mine not in the sense that you are mine but mine in the sense that I feel your pulse too I couldn't stop seeing you if I wanted to seeing your gentle kind compassionate graceful perceptive brave strong funny intelligent beautiful magikal existence that's what I mean I mean I take the responsibility of witnessing you deathly seriously I mean it is a gift of the absolute utmost immense proportions to be able to witness you I mean I know this is heavy-handed but it's true I mean it I mean it I mean it you taught me how to love you're teaching me how to love do you embrace what I mean feel it in your blood inhale it let it sustain you exhale the waste left behind it's rapturing that you may photosynthesize moonlight take action start today (again) see you're well on your way?

You're well on your way.

Unfolding Incarnate

And then again we danced,
numbers and colors becoming ours,
states of matter taking on new meaning
amongst our witticisms and
moist pleasures.
Synchronicity and synecdoche and seances and slime
calling forth that which was dead inside us -
the parts that already knew we loved one another
but didn't yet have the direction
our entanglement provided.
Spacetime surfers,
cunty comrades,
could we be any bolder in our cherishing?
I knew you when I smelled a flower for the first time.
You had me hooked before I ever saw you,
your smile a confirmation of what can only be called
fundamental:
this love, which has bloomed in every generation -
a lineage taking us back to
the hum before the Big Bang -
resurrected us from the place we are going next.
And then we died.
And then again we danced.

Schmetterling, Pt. II

after Warsan Shire

No.

No, suffering is not our calling
nor our savior.
We will not be coaxed back to the cocoon -
pain is neither our comfort nor our redemption.

There is a curse, and it has been broken.

Yes.

Yes, it is easier to see hurt,
but we choose otherwise.
This horizon,
this hope,
these unsteady flaps of newly formed wings -
it is all ours, and always has been.
Abundance is all around.
Join me here.
This horizon is meant for us.

Acknowledgments

My deepest gratitude is directed towards myself. *Let It Sustain You* is an altar to who I once was, an honoring of all the parts of myself I used to be too ashamed to claim as me. Thank you Emma, for fumbling clumsily and steadfastly towards yourself, again and again and again.

Thank you Michael. Thank you for witnessing me, for writing with me, and for imbuing me with the bravery and fortitude to live authentically. You are truly my poetic and spiritual contemporary.

Chiara, you are a visionary. Thank you for your brilliant cover design and friendship.

* * *

To Mirko a million thanks. Thank you for encouraging me, celebrating me, and turning towards the best of me even when I could only see the worst.

* * *

I am in awe of the beauty my friends conjure and reveal in

this world. Y'all are the reason I am alive today. Thank you to every one of you for teaching me the meaning of life.

I would not be who I am without the writers whose works have changed me. I am humbled by and eternally grateful for so many, with a special appreciation for the influence Ursula K. Le Guin and Audre Lorde have had on the writing in this book. I bow to them and lay flowers at their feet for expanding my world and touching me deeply.

About the Author

Emma K. Shockley likes to collect rocks, listen to the wind, and watch the light change. She is passionate about words, presence, pleasure, laughter, being well rested, and uncovering commonality.

www.ingramcontent.com/pod-product-compliance
Lightning Source LLC
LaVergne TN
LVHW041926070526
838199LV00051BA/2724